Voyage of Self Discovery

An Astrological Guide

Angel Rae

Voyage of Self Discovery An Astrological Guide

By Angel Rae

is published by Dark Moon Press

Ft. Wayne, Indiana

ISBN-13: 978-1533124906

For a full catalogue of Dark Moon's publications refer to
http://www.darkmoonpress.com

Or send an SASE to:
P.O. Box 11496, Ft. Wayne, Indiana, 46858-1496

Table of Contents

Introduction

At some point in time we have all been curious. Curious as to why we do what we do or why others do what they do. We wonder what makes us tick and why we have certain pet peeves or display the same patterns in life. We may turn to horoscopes for some kind of insight or warning about our day to come. Some of us use divination tools such as Tarot or Oracle decks. These are great tools to capture what's going on in your life or for guidance on how to deal with the things in your life.

Astrology is a wonderful tool but much different than divination, it's for a deeper look into you and the people around you! We must first discover who we are. What drives us? What holds us back? What, within our makeup, can we understand further about ourselves? Imagine the changes we could make if we were more self-aware of our personalities and patterns.

Astrology is a wonderful and fun way to explore the deeper nature of the true us. It can be used in understanding others and the way they tick. We all have light and dark sides to our personalities and astrology isn't about pointing out the bad and good, but a view into our life paths and into an awakening of our actions, reactions, and choices in life! Learning someone has a prideful or insecure characteristic can make it easier to interact with them and have a better understanding as to why they do or say things they say, which leads to compassion.

I have compiled fascinating, multi-cultural astrological information including numerology and the Major Arcana of the Tarot! I will give a brief history for each astrological chart and the beliefs behind them. This is an area that I have long been enchanted by and I am very excited to bring to you all the information I have gathered over the years. I hope it brings a better understanding of you and those around you! This is not a book on how to change yourself or others, by any means. It is a broader, more intense look into understanding people and how to best eliminate negative patterns or what characteristics to embrace.

If we understand more about a person's light and dark sides, and accept them, then it enables us to better handle, not just our personalities, but our habits and those of others we interact with. Above all else, I hope this book takes you on a personal journey to enlightenment and gives you a better understanding of you and the ones you hold near and dear!

History of Astrology

Astrology has been around for thousands of years. Tracing its roots back to ancient Babylonia, it was practiced by the priests to decipher the will of the Gods. From Babylonia, astrology was adopted by the Greeks. They trusted the stars and the oracles to forecast the future. The Hindus of India were also exploring astrology at this time, between 5000 and 3000 BC, developing some of the same signs we use today.

It was the Egyptians who first used astrology to foretell the character of a person based on their date of birth. Star charts have been discovered in Egypt dating as far back as 4300 BC. The Chinese also developed a system of astrology around 2800 BC. It has evolved very differently than Western astrology. The Greeks influenced Egyptian astrology with what they learned from the Babylonians. Ptolemy wrote a book on astrology that set down the current practice of using planets, houses, and signs.

The most famous astrologer is Nostradamus, who is said to have foreseen events such as the Second World War, the assassination of the American President John F. Kennedy, and the attack on the World Trade Centre. The Zodiac was originally a natural agricultural calendar that dated the sowing and harvesting of crops. Astrology is thought to be both a science and an art. It displays scientific attributes because it requires mathematical capabilities and knowledge of Astronomy. It is also an art because interpretation is needed to bring all the different aspects together and formulate a profile of the individual's character traits and tendencies.

Numerology and life path characteristics

Numerology is the study of numbers in a metaphysical manner in which they reflect certain characteristics and attributes and help make up our cosmic destiny. To find what your path life number is, you simply add your birthdate numbers! The life path numbers are 1 through 9 and you reduce your sum to find the single digit for your number! If your full birth date ends in an 11 or 22, those would be considered 2 (1+1) and 4 (2+2) and considered "master numbers".

As I said before, it is fairly simple to find what your life path or numerology number is. Below, you will find an example of a birthdate and how exactly we come to the equation for that date! The object is to "reduce down" enough times to reach a single digit that represents your numerology number!

Example: July 20, 1973

7+2= 9, 9+1= 10, 10+9 = 19, 19+7= 26, 26+ 3= 29-reduce down 2+9= 11, reduce down again and end up with 1+1=2

2 is this birthdate's numerology number

We will discuss all nine numbers as well as the Master numbers 11 and 22, to help you better understand what your specific number means and the connections it has with your life. Numerology is a slightly different form of astrology that we can use to delve deeper into our thoughts, actions, and reactions, involving others. Working with Tarot and numerology works hand in hand with one another because the numbers are very significant for attaining a deeper reading.

The first thing you should do is find your life path number! You can figure out the numbers of family and friends as well and read up on their life path numbers! I have discovered that the people I'm closest to have the same numerological numbers as I or are evident, in some way, within my circle. The people I had conflicts with, didn't "mesh" with or had failed relationships with, came out with different numerological patterns! I was very intrigued when I put it all together and had all those "aha" moments. So let's get started!

Numerology Life Path Numbers 1-9

1- Born leader, very competitive, successful in goal achieving, egotistical, and can be considered selfish because you put yourself first. You may have many relationships until you choose to settle down. You demand faithfulness and find it hard to forgive and forget when wronged. You would make a good athlete, politician or someone that's in the spotlight. Might suffer from headaches or eye problems. You have a strong will but if you become lazy, you will quickly put on weight which could lead to further health problems.

2- Peacemaker with a sensitivity towards others and are a great listener. Sincere, honest and open to others and will make a great lover or friend. You are usually called upon to be the "mediator" in a situation because you can look at the big picture. You can be very persuasive rather than forceful to get your point across. Many people with this life path number can be overly sensitive, shy, or afraid to speak their minds and stand up for themselves. You often deny your own needs in order to fill the needs of others which can lead to resentment or anger. Good career choices would be counseling, teaching, meditating, customer relations, poetry, arts and music, science, botany, and administrations.

3- Creative and optimistic with a high level of self-expression. You tend to live in the moment, partly because you don't like to think about your responsibilities and assume things will work out fine all on their own. You are charismatic and people like to be around you. You are a great listener and are very conscious of others emotions. You are extremely generous and enjoy living life to its fullest! You can procrastinate and probably aren't good with money and finances because you can be disorganized and careless about your responsibilities. When you are hurt, you tend to detach

4

and become very moody. Career choices for you would be a poet, actor, artist, dancer, author, musician, chef or attorney.

4- The worker bees of society! Determined, practical and hard working. You expect hard work out of others as well and are considered "down to earth". Organized and able to tackle challenges if there is a plan in order. You are set in your ways and lead a pretty simple life. You have a strong sense of right and wrong. You're honest and expect that of others as well. Loyal and very dependable and make a great friend or lover but prefers a small circle of friends. Can be stubborn, rigid, or too serious. Sometimes you can be tactless and allow your true feelings to emerge, even when people don't want to hear it. Not a risk taker and doesn't stray from the original plan. Career choices would include, engineer, architect, mathematician, mechanic, sculptor or computer whiz.

5- Seeker of freedom. Always seeking change and are an adventurous soul who is curious and looks for the meanings of life's phases. Hates routine and repetition and makes a fantastic motivational speaker for others. Extremely compassionate, and have a genuine concern for others and their freedom. If you become stuck in a mundane kind of life, you get restless and impatient. Career choices are a salesman, teacher, reporter, scientist, and investor.

6- Incredible nurturers, caretakers, and providers. Your life revolves around home and family and strong parenting instincts. You enjoy being a service to others, especially family and friends! You are understanding and compassionate. Community oriented and love helping those in need. Can be self-righteous and critical of others, and can become so caught up with the needs of others that your own needs are never met. Sometimes you can't find a balance between helping and meddling which can turn people off and can be an "enabler" due to your nurturing ways. Great careers for this path life number are a teacher, caregiver and will make a great parent. Nursing, doctor, counselor and social work could be good as well for you to pursue.

7- A thinker, a wise person and observant. You seek truth and wisdom and have the tendency to be a perfectionist. You are most comfortable by yourself and can be called a "loner". You seek a quiet and peaceful life and are very drawn to spiritual aspects of life. Your relationships suffer because you can't connect with others or feel the closeness of being around other people. You spend so much time alone that you can become inflexible and find that balance is very difficult for you. Once you commit to something you see it through until the end. Career choices for you would be a scientist, researcher, or inventor.

8- Natural leadership skills and are very ambitious and goal oriented. You have great organization skills and will do well in business. Hard worker but can become a "workaholic". You are very good with money and your work ethic makes it possible to be very wealthy. Your need to have materialistic things can become unscrupulous in your dealings and being at work so much can hurt your personal relationships with family and friends. Good judge of character and attract the right kind of people for your goals and dreams. Status is very important to you and for this reason, you may live above your means. Good career choices for this path number are politics, real estate, business, finance, law, judge, archaeology, and author.

9- Humanitarians, and an extreme sense of compassion and generosity. You are selfless and enjoy helping others, and people genuinely like you. You are friendly and give freely your money, time and energy! You can become scattered because your talents lie in so many different directions that you may find it hard to focus on just one. If you constantly pursue materialistic gains you will feel dissatisfied and become moody or sensitive. A career in the arts is best for you but also a healer, teacher, firefighter or minister would suit you well too.

The connection between us and Numerology is quite evident when you break it down. The connection between numerology and the people in our lives is a great way to find better ways to coexist with one another. As I stated before, numerology and Tarot is a great example of how this works as well! Two significant facts exist about this theory, The Major Arcana consist of 22 cards and the Minor Arcana consist of 56 cards (5+6=11) and this leads us to the Master Numbers 11 and 22.

The master number 11 is the number of self-illumination through spiritual inspiration. The number 22 is the number that brings the cosmic law into the physical and material world. Master numbers are 11, 22, 33, 44, 55 and so on and have special properties. Master numbers teach self-mastery and indicate great power but carry great responsibility. I encourage you to further your learning on this subject!

There are many ways to use to Numerology and making important decisions, for instance, picking a certain date for an important occasion and comparing the numerology date to the date you want to hold or attend the event. Picking a date that links with your life path number can ensure better results! It can help you better understand yourself and those around you in a more intimate way. Numbers have a connection to everything in the universe just as we do!

American Zodiac/Sun Signs

The term Zodiac is Greek for "animal". They divided the heavens into 12 different constellations and attributed the personalities affiliated with the nature of each sign and is considered to be your personal Sun Sign. According to the date and month in which you are born is how you find out what sign you fall under! With this information, you can then read your horoscope, find what other signs you are compatible with and possibly what kind of career or life path is more suited for you.

Our Sun Signs are doorways to our conscious lives, our personalities and the personalities of others. It can be used like a map to you and the people around you. This is a guide to our "active" and "reactive" sides and will explain why we do what we do throughout our lives. In the next chapter, we'll discuss the Moon Signs that will put that puzzle piece into place that is missing from your life, the place once you've entered after going through the doorway to your conscious being. Your unconscious fears, desires, and characteristics will be revealed once you complete the Sun Sign section!

Sun Signs

Aries: March 21st- April 19th
PLANET: MARS
POWER STONE: DIAMOND
ELEMENT: FIRE
SYMBOL: THE RAM

KEYWORDS: Active, demanding, determined, effective and ambitious

They like and seek out adventures. Aries people are risk takers and do it with a smile on their faces! They are quick to take in a situation but very quick to leave the scene. They'll be the first ones there to help save you but will show great anger towards you for putting yourself in danger, to begin with. Aries have a very "me first" mentality and come off as being very selfish and egotistical. Notorious for taking temper tantrums to get their way!

Compatible Sun Signs are: Leo, Sagittarius, Gemini, Aquarius

Least compatible sign: Cancer, Pisces, Taurus, Capricorn

Taurus: April 20th- May 20th
PLANET: VENUS
POWER STONE: EMERALD
ELEMENT: EARTH
SYMBOL: THE BULL

KEYWORDS: Security, subtle strength, appreciation, instruction and patient

Taurus people are very reliable, dependable, patient and diligent. They have a reserved quiet inner strength and are very goal oriented. They are very loyal creatures but tend to be very stubborn. They don't accept or adapt to change very well and will avoid it, if possible. Taurus people can be very secretive, stingy or suspicious of others. They love great food and are most comfortable in familiar surroundings.

Compatible Sun Signs are: Virgo, Capricorn, Cancer, Pisces

Least compatible: Gemini, Aquarius, Aries, Leo

Gemini: May 21st- June 20th
PLANET: MERCURY
POWER STONE: PEARL
ELEMENT: AIR
SYMBOL: THE TWINS

KEYWORDS: Communication, Indecision, Inquisitive, Intelligent, Changeable.

The Twins have a need to communicate their thoughts, plans, and ideas. They are very intelligent and highly adaptive creatures. They are very curious about life and its experiences. They embrace new adventures and experiences. Often they take on too many projects and tend to be dreamers. They know a little about a lot! Gemini people make explosive first impressions and are usually surrounded by a huge social circle. They can be what is considered a "suck up" to some and tell people what they want to hear instead of what they truly believe or feel.

Compatible Sun Signs are: Libra, Aquarius, Aries, Leo

Least compatible: Cancer, Pisces, Taurus, Virgo

Cancer: June 21st- July 22nd
PLANET: MOON
POWER STONE: RUBY
ELEMENT: WATER
SYMBOL: CRAB

KEYWORDS: Emotional, diplomatic, intensity, impulsive, selective

Cancer people are all about home and family. They are great nurturers and healers. Often called "the natural mother type" and are great at keeping their households in order. They can be kind, great listeners and very compassionate towards others, but not typically themselves. Crabs maintain their hard exterior shell in hopes of protecting their softer, vulnerable side. They are unpredictable people and need constant reassurance that they are loved, appreciated and needed! They tend to hold onto emotional baggage from the past and rarely forgive and forget.

Compatible Sun Signs are: Scorpio, Pisces, Taurus, Virgo

Least compatible: Aries, Leo. Gemini, Libra

Leo: July 23rd- August 22nd
PLANET: SUN
POWER STONE: PERIDOT
ELEMENT: FIRE
SYMBOL: LION

KEYWORDS: Ruling, warmth, generosity, faithful, innovative

These lions are enthusiastic and generous creatures. A real love for life and all the pleasures it has to offer. They tend to thrive on drama and demand to be in the spotlight with lots of attention. They are very affectionate and passionate with their relationships and endeavors. Great friends that are cheerful and ready to have a good time! They seek out flattery and are quite flirty themselves by being so charming. Leo's are very hard workers and take on projects most people would shy away from. They are very prideful and refuse to change themselves or their patterns for anyone. They rarely admit when they are wrong, which is never because their egos won't allow it. Most lions are playful and the life of the party in their social circles.

Compatible Sun Signs are: Aries, Sagittarius, Gemini, Libra

Least compatible: Pisces, Taurus, Scorpio

Virgo: August 23rd- September 22nd
PLANET: MERCURY
POWER STONE: SAPPHIRE
ELEMENT: EARTH
SYMBOL: THE VIRGIN

KEYWORDS: Analyzing, practical, reflective, observation, thoughtful

Virgos are the signs of service to others. Big on self-improvement and helping their loved ones become better people. They put their knowledge to practical uses and are usually successful in doing so. They demand organization in their lives and with their belongings. Striving for perfection and are not happy if not achieved! Virgos can be cynical and skeptical, which leads to unhappy relationships to self and with others. They can be shy and reserved and find it very difficult to mingle with strangers. These sun signs use logic and reason when it comes to issues and is not overly dramatic creatures. They have the ability to be sensual, passionate and cautious all at the same time.

Compatible Sun Signs are: Taurus, Capricorn, Cancer, Scorpio

Least compatible: Aquarius, Gemini, Libra

Libra: September 23rd- October 22nd
PLANET: VENUS
POWER STONE: OPAL
ELEMENT: AIR
SYMBOL: SCALES

KEYWORDS: Balance, justice, truth, beauty, perfectionist

A sign of partnership, Libras are charming individuals and love to make others feel good and important. They seek balance at all costs and strive for harmony. They are born diplomats due to their ability to see both sides of an issue. They do not like or engage in a confrontation so they tend to agree easily and be all things to all people. Libras sometimes come off as indecisive or scatter- brained. They thrive on being adored and respond well to praise and flattery. They are very creative and imaginative people but bore very easy so keep them entertained with new ideas often!

Compatible Sun Signs are: Gemini, Aquarius, Leo, Sagittarius

Least compatible: Aries, Capricorn, Cancer

Scorpio: October 23rd- November 21st
PLANET: PLUTO
POWER STONE: CITRINE
ELEMENT: WATER
SYMBOL: SCORPION

KEYWORDS: Transient, self-willed, purposeful, relentless

The sign of extremes. Scorpios embody the best and worst in human nature. Brooding, jealousy and vengeful spirit may cause issues in relationships. When positive emotions evolve, the Scorpion energy shines bright with drive and endurance. They are accomplished when taking on projects and are tenacious at getting things done.

They never forget the kindness and will repay with quite a generosity! Don't make one your enemy though, they don't forgive and forget easily and will make sure you never forget the wrongdoing. They are emotional creatures and may use guilt or manipulate others to get what they want.

Compatible Sun Signs are: Cancer, Pisces, Virgo, Capricorn

Least compatible: Aquarius, Gemini, Leo

Sagittarius: November 22nd- December 21st
PLANET: JUPITER
POWER STONE: BLUE TOPAZ
ELEMENT: FIRE
SYMBOL: CENTAUR (HALF MAN; HALF HORSE)

KEYWORDS: Philosophical, motivated, experimental, optimistic

The optimistic Sagittarius. They seem to breeze through life with great luck and many opportunities show up at the right time and right places. They are restless and independent by nature. Typically, they don't stay in long term relationships or commitments. Very direct and honest people and some may even say too blunt. They are sensitive creatures and can be hurt easily with words and actions they feel are out to be malicious. Living for today and worry about tomorrow is their motto. They can be flirtatious and charming but find passion in relationships instead of domestic bliss. Sagittarius people are the perfect "playmate" as long as you don't attempt to tie them down.

Compatible Sun Signs are: Leo, Aries, Libra, Aquarius

Least compatible: Taurus, Virgo, Cancer

Capricorn: December 22nd- January 19th
PLANET: SATURN
POWER STONE: GARNET
ELEMENT: EARTH
SYMBOL: MOUNTAIN GOAT

KEYWORDS: Determined, dominant, persevering, practical, willful

Ambitious and motivated describe our Capricorn people. They strive for money, success, and power. They are determined to succeed at all costs, no matter the price. Good sense of humor but do not appreciate ridicule or being poked fun at. Good at concealing their insecurities or denying them all together. They expect respect and admiration from others. Capricorns like to test the loyalty of their loved ones because they have a great need to be loved and appreciated. They are faithful and their passions run very deep.

Compatible Sun Signs are: Virgo, Taurus, Scorpio, Pisces

Least compatible: Aries, Leo, Gemini

Aquarius: January 20th- February 18th
PLANET: URANUS
POWER STONE: AMETHYST
ELEMENT: AIR
SYMBOL: WATER-BEARER

KEYWORDS: Knowledgeable, humanitarian, serious, insightful,

The unorthodox sign of the group. They seek to be different than everyone else. Free thinkers with a hope to do something meaningful in their endeavors. They tend to have a strong and stubborn side to them and very resistant to change. They are very loyal and kind to anyone they cross paths with. They have a magnetic personality which is why many are attracted to them almost immediately. Aquarius people stimulate their relationships by staying creative. It's when they feel trapped that problems arise. Free spirits must feel free or will flee.

Compatible Sun Signs are: Libra, Gemini, Sagittarius, Aries

Least compatible: Taurus, Capricorn, Cancer

Pisces: February 19th- March 20th
PLANET: NEPTUNE
POWER STONE: AQUAMARINE
ELEMENT: WATER
SYMBOL: FISH

KEYWORDS: Fluctuation, depth, imagination, sensitive, indecisive

Pisces are the sign of eternity. They are compassionate and fair minded people. They have great intuition but either not listen to it or second guess it. Very sensitive when being talked to but can be insensitive to others without a thought. They may fall for the "wrong ones" often because they readily think they can identify with their partner's feelings. These fish adapt well and quickly when needed. Almost all their reactions are emotionally based. They are very creative and rely on their imaginations for entertainment. Good career choices would be artists, writers, and musicians.

Compatible Sun Signs are: Scorpio, Cancer, Capricorn, Taurus

Least compatible: Aries, Leo, Gemini

Those are the 12 Sun Signs and I only touched on the basic characteristics of these signs. You can research your Sun Sign more in depth and there are many other compatibility charts specifically for Love, Career, Friendships and so on! Discovering your Moon Signs is helpful and fun too! The Moon Signs go deeper into your emotional and inner self. Sun signs are our conscious and Moon signs are our unconscious and can indicate your habits and instinctual side!

Zodiac - Moon Signs

As I stated in the previous chapter, our Moon signs are our unconscious and reflect our habits and intuition. They help define our emotional progress. Since the Moon passes through each sign so fast, the time of birth is essential! That's the tricky part to discovering your moon sign, by a chart and you'll need your time of birth! You could ask someone to write a chart up for you or simply choose one of the many moon sign calculators online!

Most people will have a different Moon sign than their Sun sign, however, if it does so happen that you have the same, your characteristics and personality traits will be more intense or amplified. If you do not know your birth time then you can calculate your birth time at 12:01 A.M. and again at 11:59 P.M., if they are the same then you have successfully discovered your Moon sign! If they are different, read both profiles and match it up to what you feel is the closest to you and your personality! By delving deeper into Moon signs, you can acquire the following:

- *Developing Intuition*

- *Emotional Behaviors*

- *Feminine Influences*

- *Instinctive Behaviors*

- *Unconscious Desires*

- *Childhood Influences*

- *Psychic Development*

- *Enhancing Receptivity*

- *Motherly Intentions*

- *Understanding Dreams*

- *Environmental Awareness*

- *Uncovering Hidden Motives*

- *Past Memory and Regression*

- *Pleasure and Sensual Preference*

Moon Signs

ARIES MOON

Not known for their self-discipline or control, they are very impulsive beings and very enthusiastic in everything they do! Their hearts rule their heads and can get them into some shady situations sometimes. Aries moon people are happy, optimistic and full of life. They seek instant gratification and don't like to wait for results in any manner. They are not subtle with people but are witty and tend to blame others when things go wrong.

Aries moons are very impatient which causes them to miss out on opportunities. These signs are ruled by their emotional needs and desires. They tend to be very dominant whether they are at work, home, or social situations. Becoming pouty or even angry if their attempts at success are not met to perfection but recover quickly and move on to gain the results they intended or wanted. Aries Moon people hide their sorrow and suffering, from themselves as well as others and don't look beyond the situation.

TAURUS MOON

Your light shines the brightest when you know exactly where you stand, whether at your job, home and relationships. Taurus moon people demand honesty above all else and feel very disrespected if they know they have been betrayed or lied to. They don't engage in mind games and will retreat if trying to be pulled into someone else's drama or games.

20

These signs tend to be sophisticated and prefer the finer things in life. They can become very depressed if they are not surrounded by beauty within their environment. Inner wisdom is a great gift that comes with the characteristics of this Moon sign! They are often right and trust their inner instincts to guide them through life.

GEMINI MOON

A very social being is one word to describe our Gemini Moon! The more friends around them, the better! Their minds are always churning and looking for something to do. They are very flexible with all that they encounter and have a "happy-go-lucky" attitude. These signs have a genuine need for interaction, they don't care what kind of interaction and normally don't care if they have to result to combativeness to get it.

Gemini Moon people are very impulsive and like to move around often, which makes them great travelers! They welcome change with open arm and encourage people to be the same. These signs are often accused of being superficial or shallow but they just know what they want and there's no room to settle for anything less. These beings have the gift to adapt to their surroundings as well as their sorrow, anxiety or stress and move on easily.

CANCER MOON

Known to positively glow when these signs are helping others! Cancer Moon people are very supportive and want the ones they love to succeed. When rewards are given or shown after working hard on a project, they can enjoy a happiness that goes very deep. They love to make a difference in all creatures' lives, human and not, and not only cherish but expect recognition for the efforts.

These signs thrive when appreciated and feeling needed is like a drug for them. They are usually great role models and even better teachers or mentors! Remarkable intuitive skills and usually accompanied by a strong psychic gift or gifts. This signs biggest issue is having the confidence to come out of their hard shell but once they do come out, people tend to see the fun, loving and kind person that the Cancer Moon is.

LEO MOON

The proud Lion! Very charming and generally happy and positive people. Leo's make great leaders and fit perfectly into a managerial position. The confidence this sign carries, along with their prideful ways, are great bosses! They give off powerful energy and make others feel a calming warmth when around them. Very generous in nature but too prideful for any handouts.

They don't take criticism well and feel degraded if things they did wrong are pointed out. Leo Moon people can be very domineering or pushy and can be a turn off for some. They are known for the loving, kind and generous hearts though and deep down they can be tamed by the right person. They are very loving, loyal and passionate lovers but can sometimes be very hypocritical. What's good for the goose is not what's good for the gander if you ask a Leo. This type of thinking can sometimes cause conflicts at work, home or within relationships because they think they deserve different rules.

VIRGO MOON

Due to their extreme awareness of their senses, Virgo Moon people are usually anxious and very uneasy or twitchy at times. They tend to absorb what's in their atmosphere and may even be considered to be an "Empath" to some people. They carefully sort out details and are very organized and feel stressed when things are in chaos or not within their control. Virgo's are can get a little irritable so they will go off alone and keep to themselves.

They have difficulty accepting things for what they are and show great impatience with life and the people around them. They are very critical of themselves and others and can push people away because of it. These signs set such high expectations for not just themselves but others and sometimes disappointment leads to feelings of failure and defeat.

LIBRA MOON

One of the kindest of all the Moon signs. Libra's are polite and well-mannered when dealing with all beings. They are very passive and will agree with others just to avoid confrontations. They can be too generous at times and cause others to take advantage of them. Their biggest lessons in life are that their desires, needs, and wants are just as important as anyone else in their life.

Libra Moon people desire harmony and a peaceful surrounding. They can be indecisive or second guess their choices and will allow someone else to take control and make the decisions. Fairness and justice are very important to this sign and is the one time they will fight to have or be known for!

SCORPIO MOON

These Moon signs thrive better in private, without watchful eyes. The intuitive abilities that come along with this sign run deep. People find themselves sharing things with them without knowing why. In order to process any chaos or obstacles, these people need alone time to ponder, regroup and reassess. These signs tend to hold onto the past or the past hurts and finds it very hard to forgive themselves and others.

Great manipulators and focused on getting what they want, when they want it! They tend to find balance even amongst their very own intense energy. They like material things and the more expensive, the better. They will use guilt as a means to get their way as well and have no shame in doing so. Scorpio's can be very generous but on their terms and are not the type to let others forget they helped them out.

SAGITTARIUS MOON

Known as the life-long student! Sagittarius Moon people are observant and alert at all times, no matter the situation and make great police officer or military careers! They are open minded and demand their freedom and understanding from people in their life. Adventurous by nature, these signs make great travelers because they're always seeking a thrill! They are lovers of nature and feel most comfortable with it.

There's always a desire for more knowledge and these Moon people are like sponges, soaking up all the wisdom they can gather. They are known for passing the wisdom around to others when the opportunity arises. They have a constant need for activity and are always on the go. These signs have a strong idea of justice and seek fairness with all their dealings.

CAPRICORN MOON
Always in control and are not happy when they lose it. Self-discipline and predictability are the dominant characteristics with Capricorn Moon people. They can appear to come off as cold or detached at times, especially if it doesn't benefit them in any way. These signs will set their minds on a project and not only finish it, but finish it to near perfection. People often say these Moon signs have the ability to make things look so easy to perform but sometimes make others feel inadequate because of their workmanship.

They are very pragmatic and like to not only plan ahead but have plans for other scenarios in case something changes. There is a mixture of patience, drive, and determination to see anything through to the end! They are dependable and consistent and people search this sign out for help and guidance.

AQUARIUS MOON
Nature lovers and sponges when it comes to new studies, in fact, they can't get enough! They often feel like the "black sheep" or just different from others but still maintain a fulfilling social life. Aquarius Moon people have strong egos and are usually driven by it. They work hard at being the best person they can be but that ego of theirs sometimes can hinder their perspective. These signs are idealistic and in a constant cycle of change or

24

progression. They can be jealous individuals and sometimes very possessive but it stems from living in fear and doubt caused by low self-esteem. Prone to having temper tantrums to get what they want whether it's a physical object or just attention! They desire freedom and don't like to feel as if they have no voice because their egos demand to be heard! Great humanitarians and very kind but can come off as detached to those who don't know them on a personal level.

PISCES MOON

The most sensitive of all the Moon signs. They exist on the darker side of the moon, so to speak. They come off as reserved or withdrawn and shy but that's just their nervous exterior, once you get to know them they are quite entertaining and love hearing and telling stories! Anxiety plays a huge role with Pisces Moon people but they can learn to control it as they get older.

They are very instinctive but rarely rely on their gut feelings because they tend to second guess themselves. Their abilities can sometimes catch them off guard and not really know how to utilize their spiritual gifts. These signs have keen observation but are not obvious about in any way. They like their privacy and tend to be secretive. One of the most creative signs in the group and depend on their imaginations to get through life, especially if they are lacking something within it. When given the freedom to do what they want, when they want they maintain a contentment with themselves as well as their relationships. Careful though, they are so sensitive that any critical remarks can just destroy them and cause them to think they are not good enough, which can lead to sadness and anger.

When you have gathered what information you wanted from the Sun Sign characteristics and Moon Sign characteristics, compare the two. Seek out how much you can identify with yourself and others and it's a wonderful way to discover the conscious and unconscious aspects of you! As progress in this book, keep track of your profiles as you go along and when you have reached the end of the book, I have complete faith you will have a better understanding what makes us tick!

When I did my profile chart for the first time, after finishing this project, it read like a story. A story of me. Stories of the people around us that hurt us, make us angry or happy. Because our Moon Signs control our unconscious, unlike other Zodiacs, I feel our Sun and Moon signs are vital to understanding or gaining that insight we desperately need and search for!

Native American Astrology

This is by far my favorite Astrological tool! Like the Chinese Zodiac, Native Americans used animals as signs of their Zodiac and focused on the characteristics of each animal as it pertains to you and your personal self. Native Americans throughout history and in present times have held a sacred connection between animals, nature, and man. Native American astrology can give insight into yourself, others around you, and your life path.

By tapping into the powers of our animal spirits, we gain a higher perspective and understanding of their role in our lives. In this chapter, I will briefly touch on other aspects for each Animal Sign but really encourage you to follow up on the animal itself and the Clans associated with your sign!

Native American signs

Goose: December 22nd- January 19th
Elemental Aspect- Earth
Elemental Clan- Turtle

Goose people are reliable, hold high self-standards, ambitious, never gives up, rigid, driven, too focused on succeeding, sociable, well spoken, self-doubt, determined, resourceful, level-headed and can be self-involved. If you want something done - give it to the Goose. Persevering, dogmatic and ambitious to a fault, the Goose sets goals for accomplishment, and always obtains them. The Goose can be very passionate, humorous, gregarious, and very sensual.

Spiritual Energy- Masculine

Compatible Signs are: Beavers, Bear, Crow

Otter: January 20th- February 18th
Elemental Aspect- Air
Elemental Clan- Butterfly

Otter people are sociable, talkative, independent, creative, unconventional, inventive, soothing, perceptive, intrusive, unpredictable, blunt, tolerant, courageous, rebellious, eccentric, friendly and tactless at times. They have an unusual way of looking at things but are equipped with a brilliant imagination and intelligence, allowing them an edge over everyone else. Often very perceptive and intuitive, the Otter makes a very good friend and can be very attentive. In a nurturing environment, the Otter is sensitive, sympathetic and honest.

Spiritual Energy- Masculine

Compatible Signs are: Crow, Falcon, Deer

Wolf: February 19th- March 20th
Elemental Aspect- Water
Elemental Clan- Frog

Wolves are compassionate, generous, artistic, gentle, sympathetic, adaptable, impressionable, sensitive, impractical, vague, timid, indecisive, psychic, intuitive, mystical, impressionable, tender, trusting, loving and can be materialistic. They believe that all we need is love, and is fully capable of providing it. In a nurturing environment, they can be intensely passionate, generous, deeply affectionate, and gentle. They can become impractical, obsessive, and vindictive on their "bad" days.

Spiritual Energy- Feminine

Compatible Signs are: Woodpeckers, Bear, Snakes

Falcon/ Hawk: March 21st- April 19th
Elemental Aspect- Fire
Elemental Clan- Hawk

Falcon people are active, quickly aroused, pioneering spirits, impatient, selfish, egotistical, persistent, patient with others, great leaders, conceited, speedy, adventurous, passionate and can be intolerant with the flaws of others. A natural born leader, the Falcon can always be looked upon for clear judgment in complex situations. Ever persistent, and always taking the initiative, the Falcon makes a great addition to any projects or team sports. They have the ability to maintain passion and fire in relationships, and always remain compassionate in nature, when interacting with others.

Spiritual Energy- Feminine

Compatible Signs- Salmon and Owl

Beaver: April 20th- May 20th
Elemental Aspect- Earth
Elemental Clan- Turtle

Beaver people are resourceful, methodical, high strung, persistent, strong-willed, inflexible, possessive, self-involved, easily accepting of change, compassionate, confident, industrious and can be oblivious when something isn't directly in front of them. Strategic, and cunning the Beaver is a force to be reckoned with in matters of business, combat, and debates. The Beaver can be understanding, generous, helpful, and loyal.

Spiritual Energy- Masculine

Compatible Signs are: Woodpeckers, Bear, Geese

Deer: May 21st- June 20th
Elemental Aspect- Air
Elemental Clan- Butterfly

Gentle deer people are talkative, congenial, moody, daydreamers, sensitive, friendly, intellectual, quick witted, restless, insecure, persistent, skilled communicators, and can be a friend to all that approach them. The Deer is inspiring, lively and quick-witted and with a great sense of humor, the Deer has a tendency to get a laugh out of anyone. They are always aware of their surroundings and even more focused on their appearance...they can be a bit self-involved.

Spiritual Energy- Feminine

Compatible Signs are: Crow and Otter

Woodpecker: June 21st- July 21st
Elemental Aspect- Water
Elemental Clan- Frog

Woodpeckers are emotional, protective, vulnerable, tender, sympathetic, moody, unforgiving, resourcefulness, self-pity, envious, dependent, sensitive, compassionate, devoted, intuitive, and can be over emotional and over nurturing to some. They want to help everyone but sometimes forget to take care of themselves. They are empathic and understanding and one sign you want to have on your side when you need support. They make wonderful parents, and equally wonderful friends and partners.

Spiritual Energy- Masculine

Compatible Signs are: Snakes, Wolf, Beaver

Salmon: July 22nd- August 21st
Elemental Aspect- Water
Elemental Clan- Fish

Salmon people are confident, energetic, passionate, intense, generous, creative, controlling, arrogant, intolerant, humbleness, letting go, egotistical, loyal and can be very prideful, especially when they are wrong. A natural motivator, the Salmon's confidence, and enthusiasm are easily infectious to others. They express a need for purpose and flock to rallies with no trouble in finding volunteers to join forces with them. Salmon are stable, calm, sensual, and giving creatures.

Spiritual Energy- Feminine

Compatible Signs are: Owl and Falcon/Hawk

Bear: August 22nd- September 22nd
Elemental Aspect- Earth
Elemental Clan- Turtle

Bear people are practical, industrious, warm, detailed, humble, trustworthy, finicky, judgmental, hypocritical, optimistic, tolerant, critical, precise, and can be very kind, once you get past the scary persona. Pragmatic, and methodical the Bear is the one to call when a steady hand is needed. The Bear's practicality and level-headedness make them an excellent business partner. They are generous with enormous hearts but are quite shy and very modest. They have the capacity for patience and temperance, which makes them excellent teachers and mentors.

Spiritual Energy- Masculine

Compatible Signs are: Geese and Beaver

Crow/Raven: September 23rd- October 22nd
Elemental Aspect- Air
Elemental Clan- Butterfly

Crow people are tolerant, friendly, diplomatic, romantic, overly optimistic, gullible, indecisive, holds grudges, cautious and can trust too easily. They are peaceful, intelligent, tricky and can be very charming to anyone they meet. Highly enthusiastic, and a natural entrepreneur, the Crow is quite a business oriented sign. They are idealistic and diplomatic and can be quite patient, and intuitive in all of their relationships. The Crow can be demanding, inconsistent, vindictive, and abrasive when they are angry.

Spiritual Energy- Feminine

Compatible Signs are: Otter and Deer

Snake: October 23rd- November 22nd
Elemental Aspect- Water
Elemental Clan- Frog

Snake people are impulsive, ambitious, discerning, imaginative, stubborn, mistrustful, creative, sensitive to others, egotistical, aloof, distant, intense, passionate, and can be scornful when their feelings are hurt. The Snake is natural in all matters of the spirit. Naturally attuned to the ethereal realm the Snake makes an excellent spiritual leader. They are quite sensitive and caring. The Snake can be passionate, inspiring, humorous, and helpful but they can also be despondent, violent, and prone to abnormal mood swings.

Spiritual Energy- Masculine

Compatible Signs are: Woodpeckers and Wolf

Owl: November 22nd- December 21st

Elemental Aspect- Fire

Elemental Clan- Hawk

Owl people are loving, independent, caring, adaptable, trustworthy, loud, restless, optimistic, happy, focused, exaggerators, concerned with status, insightful, and can be very direct. Warm, caring and natural, with an easy-going nature, the Owl is a friend to the world. The Owl can be reckless, careless, and thoughtless. They make for great artists and loves good conversations. They can be sensitive, enthusiastic, and attentive listeners but can also be excessive, overindulgent, bitter, and belligerent.

Spiritual Energy- Feminine

Compatible Signs are: Falcon/Hawk and Salmon

Animal Birth Totems play an extremely important part in Native American Astrology. In some ways resembling the Western American Sun Signs we read about in the previous chapter but adding a unique twist! We can learn to use the strengths of our Birth Signs to overcome our weaknesses and fears.

I advise that you dig deeper into your Animal Birth Totem, read on the individual characteristics of the actual animal. See if there is something about that particular animal that you see in you! Is there something about that creature that can help you with goals or hinder them? Many avenues can be taken by using all of the Zodiac tools we have at our fingertips!

Chinese Astrology

Known as Sheng Xiao is based on a twelve-year cycle and is associated with a particular animal. The animals are Rat, Ox, Tiger, Rabbit, Dragon, Snake, Horse, Sheep, Monkey, Rooster, Dog and Pig. Later in this chapter, we'll go over what each animal symbolizes and what the personal characteristics are for each sign.

The selection and order of these animals were originated by The Han Dynasty and based upon each animal's characteristics and living habits. Legends have it that the Gods ordered that the animals were to be called upon, and as they showed up in order their number would make up the Chinese Zodiac. Another legend is that the Rat rode upon the Ox until they got to their destinations and the Rat scurried off the Ox to become the first in the zodiac order!

Rat

02/18/1912-02/05/1913

02/05/1924-01/23/1925

01/24/1936-02/10/1937

02/10/1948-01/28/1949

01/28/1960-02/14/1961

02/15/1972-02/02/1973

02/02/1984-02/19/1985

02/19/1996-02/06/1997

02/06/2008-01/25/2009

01/25/2020-02/11/2021

02/11/2032-01/30/2033

01/30/2044-02/16/2045

Rats are smart and wealthy people and will work for success! Very adaptable and getting along well with others! Flair for cleanliness and tidiness, clever, adorable, personable, and materialistic. By nature, they are thoughtful, sensible, and curious creatures. In the negative, they are timid and have a lack of concentration and stability. They seek courage, responsibilities, and introspection. Not a good leader. Guided only by their interests. They have natural goodness but can appear impolite. They are likely to speculate and they see their greed as a value.

Ox

02/06/1913-01/25/1914

01/24/1925-02/12/1926

02/11/1937-01/30/1938

01/29/1949-02/16/1950

02/15/1961-02/04/1962

02/03/1973-01/22/1974

02/20/1985-02/08/1986

02/07/1997-01/27/1998

01/26/2009-02/13/2010

02/11/2021-01/31/2022

01/31/2033-02/18/2034

02/17/2045-02/05/2046

Ox people are persistent, simple, honest, and straightforward. Honest, industrious, patient, and cautious. Great leaders with a strong devotion to work and staying in power. Women are usually good wives who pay attention to their children's education. Tenderhearted people but can have a quick temper. Conservative and traditional. Poor communicators, and can be prudish and distant. Stubborn and set in their ways.

Tiger

01/26/1914-02/13/1915

02/13/1926-02/01/1927

01/31/1938-02/18/1939

02/17/1950-02/05/1951

02/05/1962-01/24/1963

01/23/1974-02/10/1975

02/09/1986-01/28/1987

01/28/1998-02/15/1999

02/14/2010-02/02/2011

02/01/2022-01/21/2023

02/19/2034-02/07/2035

Tiger people are brave, cruel, forceful and terrifying. Are symbols of power and lordliness. Tolerant, staunch, valiant, and respected. They thrive on challenges and speed and are good at expressing themselves. Can be frank and easy to win over others with trust. Most women born under the Tiger sign are intelligent, faithful and virtuous. They will protect themselves before others. Deep thinkers and capable of great sympathy, however, they can be short-tempered. Tend to be conflictive with seniors and authority figures. Hasty minds and poor decision makers. Over confident and fail in cooperation with others.

Rabbit

02/14/1915-02/02/1916

02/02/1927-01/22/1928

02/19/1939-02/08/1940

02/06/1951-01/26/1952

01/25/1963-02/12/1964

02/11/1975-01/30/1976

01/29/1987-02/16/1988

02/16/1999-02/04/2000

02/03/2011-01/22/2012

01/22/2023-02/09/2024

02/08/2035-01/27/2036

01/26/2047-02/13/2048

Rabbits display hope, tenderness, and love. Speed, distance, and stimulation, gentle, sensitive, compassionate, amiable, modest and merciful are other words that could describe this friendly sign. Great communicators with added comic relief when things get too serious. Good at creating romantic space when needed. Soft spoken and welcoming. Avoids confrontation. They are homebodies, hospitable, and very efficient. They won't push things and don't get angered easily. They can lack meditative abilities due to their lack of focus and often sink into failed financial endeavors. Soft in appearance and stubborn on the inside. They are not good at delving deep and will likely try to escape reality.

Dragon

02/03/1916-01/22/1917

01/23/1928-02/09/1929

02/09/1940-01/26/1941

01/27/1952-02/13/1953

02/13/1964-02/01/1965

01/31/1976-02/17/1977

02/17/1988-02/05/1989

02/05/2000-01/23/2001

01/23/2012-02/09/2013

02/10/2024-01/25/2025

01/28/2036-02/14/2037

Dragons represent authority, dignity, honor, success, lucky and high capacity. Lively, intellectual, energetic, and excitable. Leaders who like perfection. Not discouraged easily. Romantic and sensitive about their reputation. Great ambition and ingenious. The despise gossip and slander and are not afraid of difficulties. Hate to be used or controlled by others. Can be arrogant and impatient. Dragon women can be overconfident and unable to control their moods easily. Can be tactless, fiery, intolerant and unrealistic. They seldom give true love. Critical of others and can be in many disappointing relationships.

Snake

01/23/1917-02/10/1918

02/10/1929-01/29/1930

01/27/1941-02/14/1942

02/14/1953-02/02/1954

02/02/1965-01/20/1966

02/18/1977-02/06/1978

02/06/1989-01/26/1990

01/24/2001-02/11/2002

02/10/2013-01/30/2014

01/29/2025-02/16/2026

02/15/2037-02/03/2038

Good tempered and skills at communication with saying very little. Gracious morality and wisdom. Usually financially secure and never worry about money. A great amount of sympathy for others and tend to help out the less fortunate. They are determined and accomplished in their goals and aspirations. Appear calm on the surface, but can be intense and passionate. Women under the Snake sign tend to do well with housework but are easily irritated. Can be jealous creatures and very suspicious. They tend to overdo things and prefer to rely on themselves. Polite, headstrong and fickle at times.

Horse

02/11/1918-01/31/1919

01/30/1930-02/16/1931

02/15/1942-02/04/1943

02/03/1954-01/23/1955

01/21/1966-02/08/1967

02/07/1978-01/27/1979

01/27/1990-02/14/1991

02/12/2002-01/31/2003

01/31/2014-02/18/2015

02/17/2026-02/05/2027

02/04/2038-01/23/2039

Horse people display ingenious communication skills. Love to be in the spotlight and are very clever. Kind to others and can be quite talkative. Cheerful, perceptive, talented and stubborn. They seek entertainment and large crowds. Popular among friends and are active in their careers. Don't like to be constrained, are hot blooded and impatient. Independent and rarely listen to anyone's advice. Strong endurance but with a bad temper. Flamboyant by nature and can be wasteful. Frequently fail to finish projects on their own.

Sheep

02/01/1919-02/19/1920

02/17/1931-02/05/1932

02/05/1943-01/24/1944

01/24/1955-02/11/1956

02/09/1967-01/29/1968

01/28/1979-02/15/1980

02/15/1991-02/03/1992

02/01/2003-01/21/2004

02/19/2015-02/07/2016

02/06/2027-01/25/2028

01/24/2039-02/11/2040

Tender, polite, clever and kind-hearted. Take a liking to art and beauty. Have faith in a particular religion and a special fondness for peaceful living. They are wise, gentle and compassionate. Economical and cautious with finances. Women born under the Sheep take good care of others. Worriers who are shy, pessimistic, moody, indecisive, over sensitive, and weak willed. Timid by nature and like to be looked after by others. They thrive on flattery, compliments, and suggestions from friends and colleagues. They do not express their love openly and usually have a flair for the paranormal.

Monkey

02/20/1920-02/07/1921

02/06/1932-01/25/1933

01/25/1944-02/12/1945

02/12/1956-01/30/1957

01/30/1968-02/16/1969

02/16/1980-02/04/1981

02/04/1992-01/22/1993

01/22/2004-02/08/2005

02/08/2016-01/27/2017

01/26/2028-02/12/2029

02/12/2040-01/31/2041

Lively, flexible, quick-witted, and versatile. They love sporadic movement and are either athletic or love sports. Being talented problem solvers, they are self-assured, sociable creatures and innovative. They have a strong desire for knowledge and have exceptional memories. They do not like being controlled and have a strong desire to present themselves. Can be very creative in their careers. They like a challenge and can be disappointed if something comes too easily. They are jealous, suspicious, cunning, selfish and arrogant at times. They tend to look down upon others and be judgmental. If they are not impatient and mouthy, they can gain a great achievement.

Rooster

02/08/1921-01/27/1922

01/26/1933-02/13/1934

02/13/1945-02/01/1946

01/31/1957-02/17/1958

02/17/1969-02/05/1970

02/05/1981-01/24/1982

01/23/1993-02/09/1994

02/09/2005-01/28/2006

01/28/2017-02/15/2018

02/13/2029-02/02/2030

02/01/2041-01/21/2042

Deep thinkers and honest, bright, good communicators, ambitious, and warm hearted. They have great self-respect and seldom rely on others. Most Roosters are born very attractive and they prefer to dress up. They are quick minded and hot tempered. They like to be busy and neat. Tend to be excited quickly but soon will get bored. They are critical and think they are always right. Their emotions swing from a very high to a very low. They can be positive but very selfish and too outspoken. They are narrow-minded and vain. Like to refuse suggestions but like to lecture others.

Dog

01/28/1922-02/15/1923

02/14/1934-02/03/1935

02/02/1946-01/21/1947

02/18/1958-02/07/1959

02/06/1970-01/26/1971

01/25/1982-02/12/1983

02/10/1994-01/30/1995

01/29/2006-02/17/2007

02/16/2018-02/04/2019

02/03/2030-01/22/2031

01/22/2042-02/09/2043

Straight forward character. Faithful, courageous, dexterous, smart, and warm hearted. They know how to keep secrets and inspire other people's confidence. Great leaders at home and in their careers. They can be very stubborn but for the right reasons. Most women under this sign are appealing but lack stability. They can be cold emotionally and sometimes distant. They can find fault with many things and are noted for their sharp tongues. They are irritable and usually are bothered by unwarranted anxiety. They sometimes try to flaunt and be brave.

Pig

02/16/1923-02/04/1924

02/04/1935-01/23/1936

01/22/1947-02/09/1948

02/08/1959-01/27/1960

01/27/1971-02/24/1972

02/13/1983-02/01/1984

01/31/1995-02/18/1996

02/18/2007-02/06/2008

02/05/2019-01/24/2020

01/23/2031-02/10/2032

02/09/2043-01/29/2044

Honest and frank. Chivalrous and gallant creatures. They have a calm appearance and strong heart. They are tolerant and optimistic, but not until they become your friend. Quick tempered but hates arguments and confrontation. They are kind to their loved ones. They don't shy away from difficulties and problems. Great sleepers and very intuitive.

There are no accurate dates for the origin of the Chinese Zodiac but legend tells it that The Golden Emperor first introduced the Zodiac sometime around 2600 B.C. The year of the person's birth is considered the primary factor in Chinese Zodiac Signs and discovering your characteristics. Events and occurrences that exist in a given year are influenced by the nature of that year's animal!

Animals play a huge role in certain Zodiac charts just as they play big roles within some religions and beliefs. Animal Guides and Totem Spirit Animals for instance, or Familiars and Dream Guides are just a few ways to rely on the power of certain animals! When you discover what your "Animalities" are for each Zodiac section, dig deeper into the spiritual significance for each animal and you can expand your birth sign chart even further!

Celtic Animal and Tree Zodiac

Celtic Astrology was created by the Druids sometime around 1000 BC. The Druid religion was based on 3 basic strands of belief: the first was to remember their ancestors and the past; the second was to have an understanding of nature so that they could work with it, not against it; and the third was to explore the connection of everyday reality with that of the spiritual realm.

Most cultures have a different group of animals or symbols for each cycle within our lives and this holds true with Celtic Astrology as well. Native American Zodiac and culture will be different from Greek or Celtic astrology but a strong connection to nature nonetheless. The Celtic Zodiac is known for its mystical side and affinity to nature. Each animal had a specific quality and characteristic and over time, these attributes and traits evolved into specific meanings the Celts associated with each type of animal.

The Celtic Animal Sign is an extension of you and your habits or patterns. It provides a deeper insight into your personalities and behaviors. Unlike the Zodiac charts we have encountered thus far in the book, have been based on a twelve month or birth sign system. The Celtic Zodiac consists of 13 as well as the Celtic Tree Zodiac.

The Celts use the cycles of the moon so the year is broken into 13 months, containing 28 days each cycle. There is one extra day which is commonly referred to as "Nameless day". This day falls outside the lunar calendar and represents the unshaped potential of all things, similar to the Fool card of Tarot and the blank stone that has been added to modern rune systems.

Celtic Animal Signs

Stag/Deer
December 24th- January 20th

Stags have high ideals and aspirations. They are quick to help others with their projects which make them quite handy. They stay focused on their targets and it takes a lot to distract them. They are very prideful creatures and hold themselves as if royalty. Stags believe in hard work and their integrity is their hallmark. They are incredibly honest, patient, thorough and persistent.

Cat
January 21st- February 17th

Cat people are great observers. They have senses they can tap into to see true intentions or motivations of others. They tend to see things in a different light. Catching details most people would miss, which gives them an advantage. Cats are very creative and use their imaginations to show just how creative they can be. Very kind and intelligent creatures but sometimes come off as detached, but they are just in their own little worlds. They are quick minded and witty with excellent reasoning skills. They have the best intentions towards others and never wish harm on anyone.

Snake
February 18th- Match 17th

Very persuasive creatures. If there's a great cause or rallying of the masses, you can count on the snake to be there. They are curious and observant by nature. Those who hold the snake as their sign, hold very special traits like being great communicators and very passionate people. They can be spontaneous as well as unpredictable and never really know when and if they are going to "strike". They demand things to go their way and can become uncooperative when they are losing control. Quick-tempered and those who think to provoke them would find it was an unwise choice.

Fox
March 18th- April 14th

The Fox seems to uphold the same symbolism or reputation in most cultures. Sneaky, cunning and sly are just some of the terms used to describe Fox people. To be so cunning, one must be intelligent, patient and have plenty of room to work. The fox has such an intense energy and spirit that they are not often "tamed". They show great courage in uncomfortable situations and are very diligent. They are great story-tellers but good luck in figuring out if it's all true or not! Fox people are tender-hearted creatures but often come off as the "class clown". They are very loyal if you are lucky enough to be in their lives.

Bull/Cow
April 15th- May 12th

Bulls are strong, loving and stable individuals. Sympathetic, compassionate and honest are some of the traits of the Bull. They are great at reading others and can spot a liar from out of a lineup. Often misunderstood, Bull people can come off as moody, grumpy and very sensitive. They are the most stubborn creatures out of the all the signs and are usually not shy about admitting it. They require being surrounded by the finer things in life and if they aren't, can become gloomy and dismal. They are very loyal and trustworthy and tend to have many friends. They are well known for protecting those they love and hold dear.

Seahorse
May 13th- June 9th

Flexible, resourceful and adaptable are just some of the wonderful traits of the Seahorse. They are very clever and often called witty creatures. They tend to make great lovers for they thrive on being loved and giving it. Though seahorse people are intelligent, they stray from making others feel any less than. They have infinite memories and at times are hard to follow because they are very sharp creatures and move quickly when they have a plan or idea. Full of charisma and have the tendency to make others forget their woes.

Wren

June 10th- July 7th-

Wren people are those who you want around in a crisis. Always full of insights that others may be blind to. They are natural caregivers and don't hesitate to cheer their friends and family up when they're down. They perform best in private surroundings and without distractions. Wren people pride themselves on their responsible nature and high-integrity. They seek balance in every aspect of their lives and demand an equal share of work and play. They tend to have "Sunny" dispositions and usually have a smile on their faces. This sign makes great business owners and not just for being self-motivated but really know how to talk to people and people usually take a quick liking to them too. They prefer to live life without a care in the world.

Horse

July 8th- August 4th

Exuberant and powerful are the first words that can describe and dominate this sign. Horse people are naturally competitive because they are sure of their talents and know they'll find success. Amazing strategist and make great navigators for they have a built-in compass to rely on. They are often caught being very flirtatious and charming which attracts many love interests. They do very well with leadership roles and thrive to be at the top. Known to charge right in and take control of any situation, with confidence and authority, ending in successful results. Horse people don't mind being a part of a team instead of taking the lead but expect recognition for their efforts. They look at challenges with a smile on their faces and courage in their hearts.

Salmon

August 5th- September 1st

Salmon people tend to be introverts by choice. They are deep thinkers, always looking for answers to complex questions. They insist on alone time to ponder and dwell on their thoughts. They are unique creatures and embrace the unexplained or paranormal occurrences around them. Salmon are very intuitive and often rely on their "gut instincts" to make most of their life's choices. Naturally artistic and lean towards art, poetry, photography or music careers. The rest of the world just needs the patience to wait on any masterpieces the Salmon come up with. They have rather dreamy perspectives on life and others enjoy them because their words are generally from kind and compassionate hearts.

Swan
September 2nd- September 29th

Spiritually evolved and quite "magical", are the Swan people. They have extremely high standards and know what they like and what they want. They can see the beauty in most things that others ignore. Refined, noble and sometimes comes off as detached or cold but in reality, Swan people are very passionate about all their relationships. Spiritual growth and constant transformation are big priorities in their lives. They pay great attention to detail because they are natural observers of their surroundings. They practice reserved emotions but do not mistake hidden from extinct.

Butterfly
September 30th- October 27th

The phrase, "social butterfly" was no doubt created for this sign. They are gentle and caring creatures as long as they're not tied down. They yearn for the freedom to fly and do their own thing. Well known for being dreamers and have the purest intent within their world of dreams. They befriend easily but may not always be loyal and stick around in people's lives, but never doubt that they care. They'll return and make things happen as if they had never left. They are naturally empathetic and would never do anything to hurt anyone or anything.

Wolf
October 28th- November 24th

Wolves are very powerful creatures. They will go to great lengths to get their point across. They are fearless, brave and unwilling to budge on principal. Wolf people are the individuals wanted on the front lines and in the heat of the battle. They do not back down and have endless amounts of energy. They thrive when facing challenges and embrace the thought of a chance to be the victor. The "lone wolf" does apply with this sign but they also roam in packs and are very loyal to those who they consider family. Their stubbornness can be their strength and their weakness, depending on the situation. They ultimately get their way eventually, whether the results are good or bad.

Hawk
November 25th- December 23rd-

Hawk people can see from a much larger perspective than other signs. They can spot targets miles away and are patient enough to know when it's time to attack. If there isn't anything to throw full passion into, these signs can become scattered and unorganized. Jumping from project to project, they keep themselves quite busy. They are very open to new ideas, thoughts, and beliefs but tend to revert back to their old ways of thinking and patterns. They seek wisdom and enjoy sharing that wisdom with others. Hawk people have a keen sense of balance and navigate through life with an internal compass. They are strongly opinionated but can be persuaded with the right challenge or debate.

Celtic Tree Signs
Birch Tree
December 24th - January 20th

They love to take chances and are highly motivated to achieve their goals. They are always striving for higher aspirations to better their lives. They are natural-born leaders who know how to charm a crowd. Often taking command when a situation calls for leadership and can be quite charming. They are most compatible with Vine and Willow trees.

Rowan Tree
January 21st- February 17th

The philosophers and intellectuals and are very passionate. Born with huge imaginations and creative minds and have the ability to change things around to their advantage. They are often misunderstood, nonetheless. Others look to them for their unique perspective on life. Their inner passions provide inner motivation and self-confidence to sail through life. They are most compatible with Ivy and Hawthorn trees.

Ash Tree
February 18th- March 17th

The artist. Ash people use the beauty they see in nature to inspire them to create magnificent works of art. They have a magnetic personality and inspire others with their artistic talents. They are very intuitive and can excel in writing, art, poetry, music or science. They are free thinkers as well as imaginative and very intuitive. They are most compatible with Reed and Willow trees.

Alder Tree
March 18th- April 14th-

Very confident and friendly creatures. They are natural "social butterflies" and tend to have many friends and acquaintances. They can be advocates for a cause or project, rally the troops then lead the way for others to follow and support them. Alder people get along with everybody and everybody loves to hang around with them. They are confident and have strong moral convictions. They are most compatible with Birch and Oak trees.

Willow Tree
April 15th- May 12th-

They are highly creative, intuitive and psychic people. Willow people have a realistic and logical perspective of things that causes them to be more patient than most tree signs. They have the ability to hold vast amounts of information just from memory. They make great counselors, teachers, and advisors, which brings success in their careers and relationships. They are most compatible with Ivy and Birch trees.

Hawthorne Tree
May 13th- June 9th

They may look one way on the outside, but seem very different once you get to know them. They are well adjusted and can adapt to most life situations well - making themselves content and comforting others at the same time. Hawthorne people have a healthy sense of humor and a clear understanding of irony with a born curiosity that would make most cats jealous! They are compatible with Ash and Rowan trees.

Oak Tree
June 10th- July 7th

They have a special gift of strength and are very protective people and often become an advocate for those who do not have a voice. Oak people radiate with confidence and naturally assume everything will work out with positive results. They are wise, with a positive outlook on life and tend to thrive and enjoy large families. They are most compatible with Reed, Ash and Ivy trees.

Holly Tree
July 8th- August 4th

Positions of power and authority. They use their energy to stay focused on achieving their goals. They are generous, intelligent and confident in their abilities. Holly people are noble, intelligent, and find it easy to take on positions of leadership and power. They are competitive and ambitious even in the most casual situations and are quite generous, kind and affectionate. They can appear to be arrogant but are just very confident in their abilities. They are most compatible with Ash and Elder trees.

Hazel Tree
August 5th- September 1st

Very ambitious people that excel in academics. They are intelligent and will be attracted to careers in teaching and writing. They have great memories and are able to repeat things with stunning accuracy. Hazel people can be perfectionists and use it to their advantage within their careers. They are organized and helpful. They have an eye for detail and insist on things to be without flaw. Sometimes this need for order and control can lead to compulsive behaviors. You have a gift for numbers, science and things that utilize your analytical skills. They are most compatible with Hawthorne and Rowan trees.

Vine Tree
September 2nd- September 29th

They are born within the autumn equinox, which makes their personality changeable and unpredictable. They are able to see both sides of a situation and understand both sides equally. They are very poised and charming and have very refined tastes and love to experience the finer things in life. Vine people are charming, elegant, and maintain a level of class that wins you a loyal following from a large fan base. They are most compatible with Willow and Hazel trees.

Ivy Tree
September 30th- October 27th

They have sharp intellects and can overcome obstacles easily. Ivy people often display compassion and loyalty to others. They have giving natures and are always there to lend a helping hand to those in need. They have a tendency to be deeply spiritual and connect to a deep-rooted faith that aids them during diversity. Often soft-spoken, witty and displays empathy in most situations. They are great communicators, make good friends and are positive people to be around. They are compatible with Oak and Ash trees.

Reed Tree
October 28th- November 24th-

Discovering the hidden truths in all things are always a high priority for Reed people. They love to search for the hidden cause of things and will investigate until they find the answers they seek. Naturally good at making others feel comfortable enough to open up about themselves and usually is a keeper of secrets. They make great historians, journalists or private investigators, due to their need to know all the details. They are compatible with Ash or Oak trees.

Elder Tree
November 25th- December 23rd

They are freedom-loving and sometimes appear to be a bit wild compared to the other signs. Often misjudged as an outsider, Elders have a tendency to be withdrawn in spite of their extroverted nature. They tend to be very considerate of others and genuinely strive to be helpful. They love to be challenged mentally and thrive on constant change. They are outspoken and are considered brutally honest. They are compatible with Alder and Holly trees.

Druids believed trees were sacred and had magical and spiritual qualities. The magical qualities of trees come from the shamanic alphabet, the Ogham. The Celtic people possessed a natural attunement to the forces of Mother Nature, the cycles, creatures, and environment. As such the trees, moons and animals all played a significant part in both the mythology and the daily lives of these ancient peoples.

This relationship with Mother Nature was used to discover the internal feelings of the individual and to guide them through their life cycle. The system of Celtic tree astrology was developed out of a natural connection with the druid's knowledge of earth cycles and their reverence for the sacred knowledge held by trees.

Tarot & Astrology

The Tarot is at the top of all wisdom-seeking systems because of its diversity. This is largely due to it incorporates so many other forms of symbolism and esoteric reading systems. Numerology, archetypes, symbolic imagery and astrology types are all considered while working with the Tarot. For a more in-depth explanation of Tarot and how to do readings, pick up my book Tarot: A Deeper Journey! A great book for the beginner or professional reader!

Each of the major Arcana cards corresponds with the stars, moons, and planets within the zodiac. Tarot and astrology are two very powerful divination tools and their combination can provide profound insight to your readings. For now, though, we'll be discussing the link between the Major Arcana and the twelve zodiac correspondences.

Tarot and zodiac signs

The Emperor
Aries- March 21st- April 19th

Keywords: Active, Demanding, Determined, Effective, Ambitious

This sign will always be there when you need them. This card represents your sign's loyalty and ability to stick by your friends through thick and thin. Like the royal figure on your card, you use your authority and analytical powers to help others and yourself achieve goals.

The Hierophant
Taurus- April 20th- May 20th

Keywords: Security, Subtle strength, Appreciation, Instruction, Patience

This sign represents learning from wise teachers who can help you search for higher truths by exploring tried and true traditions. Weeding through the superficial, these old souls can lead you to the heart of matters where profound insights reveal important life lessons.

The Lovers
Gemini- May 21st- June 20th

Keywords: Communication, Indecision, Inquisitive, Intelligent, Changeable

Geminis are gifted and with a dual-natured personality that can be switched back and forth at will. Your biggest quest is often making moral choices between taking the high or low road and distinguishing between right and wrong. It's always a good idea for you to weigh your options carefully and follow the path dictated by your personal integrity and not just what you want.

The Chariot
Cancer- June 21st- July 22nd

Keywords: Emotion, Diplomatic, Intensity, Impulsive, Selective

You stand proud and strong in all your endeavors and rise above any obstacles that come your way. You seek security but love the freedom of the open road where you can use your highly-developed intuition to win the race. You have to stay busy and keep moving or your mental state suffers because you end up thinking too much and get overwhelmed.

Strength
Leo- July 23rd- August 22nd

Keywords: Ruling, Warmth, Generosity, Faithful, Initiative

This sign is the epitome of physical and mental strength. You have the courage, will, and ambition to overcome any emotional, mental or spiritual challenges. You have the ability to use compassion and understanding to soothe the "savage beast" within yourself and those around you.

Hermit
Virgo- August 23rd- September 22nd

Keywords: Analyzing, Practical, Reflective, Observation, Thoughtful

You often need to slow down and go deep within to focus on your purpose in life. The Hermit represents a person who is weary of the outer world and craves solidarity. When he retreats to explore the mysteries of his inner life, he becomes open and innocent like a child. Invests time in self-reflection and transformation.

Justice
Libra- September 23rd- October 22nd

Keywords: Balance, Justice, Truth, Beauty, Perfection

Finding yourself in situations where you need to decipher between your desires and your needs. To achieve a reasonable and fair outcome, you must put your feelings and emotions aside and look at situations rationally. You insist on everyone getting a fair shake at life's desires and will encourage those who aren't motivated in thinking so.

Death
Scorpio- October 23rd- November 21st

Keywords: Transient, Self-Willed, Purposeful, Unyielding, Tactless

You not only embrace transformation but encourage others to do so as well. You often shed your skin like a snake, seeking to release your spirit and be reborn. You are able to detach yourself from the ties that bind others to you and it's easy for you to change your identity, making you the secretive person everyone wants to figure out. You work best in private quarters and away from prying eyes.

Temperance
Sagittarius- November 22nd- December 21st

Keywords: Philosophical, Motion, Experimentation, Optimism

You are a talented mediator, able to find common ground by balancing out judgments with genuine understanding and awareness. With a balanced perspective, you work your way through whatever difficulties get in the way. Your friends and family look to you for positive advice and solutions because they know they'll always get an honest, balanced and fair answer.

The Devil
Capricorn- December 22nd- January 19th

Keywords: Determination, Dominance, Perseverance, Practical, Willful

You have the ability to face your shadow-self in order to gather the knowledge necessary for spiritual transformation and enlightenment. It's a card of self- reflection. You have the capabilities to banish any negativity that has made you doubt yourself and exchange it for confidence to be truly who you are. Self-doubt, fear, and insecurity come with this zodiac sign but as long as you are aware, you can fight those demons off.

The Star
Aquarius- January 20th-February 18th

Keywords: Knowledge, Humanitarian, Serious, Insightful, Duplicitous

This card focuses on your optimism. When you wish upon the stars, you really believe you can attain your heart's desires. Your job in this world is to convince others they can too, thereby helping to lead them on the right path, spiritually. People love being around you because of your positive energy and you attract many friends.

The Moon
Pisces- February 19th- March 20th

Keywords: Depth, Imagination, Reactive, Indecisive, Sensitive, Flexible

You are a creature of ever-changing moods, like riding a wave and above water and happy or sinking deep into the depths of sadness. There's usually no meeting in the middle, you're either up or down, emotionally. You do best when you attune to nature's cycles and use them to regenerate your intuitive powers. The Moon rules emotions, which can either be your strong suit or your downfall.

I hope you have enjoyed this astrological journey with me and encourage you to make profile charts. Start at Numerology and work your way down the list for yourself as well as others and they'll give you a deeper understanding of our human natures and characteristics! Embrace the "A-Ha!" moments and above all, have fun!

Blessed Be.

About the Author

Angel Rae comes from a small town in Pennsylvania and a long line of Spiritualists. A life-long student of Esoteric and Metaphysical practices, she encourages her readers to delve deeper and search within to find ways to transform and always strive for a better life!

Made in the USA
Middletown, DE
29 September 2020